Cursive Handwriting Workbook
This Book Belongs To:

ALPHABET A TO Z
Color the drawing and trace the letter

a=Apple

a a a a a a a a a a

a a a a a a a a a a a a a a a

a

ALPHABET A TO Z
Color the drawing and trace the letter

a=apple

a a a a a a a a a a a

a a a a a a a a a a a a a a a a a a a

a

ALPHABET A TO Z
Color the drawing and trace the letter

B=Banana

ALPHABET A TO Z
Color the drawing and trace the letter

b=banana

b b b b b b b b b b b

b b b b b b b b b b b b b b b b b b

b

Color the drawing and trace the letter

C=Carrot

C C C C C C C C C C C C

c c c c c c c c c c c c c c c

c

ALPHABET A TO Z
Color the drawing and trace the letter

c = carrot

c c c c c c c c c c c c c c

c c c c c c c c c c c c c c c c c c c

c

ALPHABET A TO Z

Color the drawing and trace the letter

D=Desk

$\mathcal{D}$ $\mathcal{D}$ $\mathcal{D}$ $\mathcal{D}$ $\mathcal{D}$ $\mathcal{D}$ $\mathcal{D}$ $\mathcal{D}$

$\mathcal{D}$ $\mathcal{D}$ $\mathcal{D}$ $\mathcal{D}$ $\mathcal{D}$ $\mathcal{D}$ $\mathcal{D}$ $\mathcal{D}$ $\mathcal{D}$ $\mathcal{D}$ $\mathcal{D}$ $\mathcal{D}$

$\mathcal{D}$

ALPHABET A TO Z
Color the drawing and trace the letter

d=desk

d d d d d d d d d

d d d d d d d d d d d d d d d d d d

d

ALPHABET A TO Z
Color the drawing and trace the letter

$\mathcal{E} = \mathcal{E}ggplant$

$\mathcal{E}$ $\mathcal{E}$ $\mathcal{E}$ $\mathcal{E}$ $\mathcal{E}$ $\mathcal{E}$ $\mathcal{E}$ $\mathcal{E}$ $\mathcal{E}$ $\mathcal{E}$

$\mathcal{E}$ $\mathcal{E}$ $\mathcal{E}$ $\mathcal{E}$ $\mathcal{E}$ $\mathcal{E}$ $\mathcal{E}$ $\mathcal{E}$ $\mathcal{E}$ $\mathcal{E}$ $\mathcal{E}$ $\mathcal{E}$ $\mathcal{E}$ $\mathcal{E}$ $\mathcal{E}$

$\mathcal{E}$

ALPHABET A TO Z
Color the drawing and trace the letter

e=eggplant

e e e e e e e e e e e e

e e e e e e e e e e e e e e e e e e e e

e

ALPHABET A TO Z
Color the drawing and trace the letter

$\mathcal{F}$=Flower

$\mathcal{F}$ $\mathcal{F}$ $\mathcal{F}$ $\mathcal{F}$ $\mathcal{F}$ $\mathcal{F}$ $\mathcal{F}$ $\mathcal{F}$ $\mathcal{F}$ $\mathcal{F}$

$\mathcal{F}$ $\mathcal{F}$ $\mathcal{F}$ $\mathcal{F}$ $\mathcal{F}$ $\mathcal{F}$ $\mathcal{F}$ $\mathcal{F}$ $\mathcal{F}$ $\mathcal{F}$ $\mathcal{F}$ $\mathcal{F}$ $\mathcal{F}$ $\mathcal{F}$

$\mathcal{F}$

ALPHABET A TO Z
Color the drawing and trace the letter

f = flower

f f f f f f f f f f f f f f

f f f f f f f f f f f f f f f f f f f f f f f f f

f

Color the drawing and trace the letter

G = Gift

ALPHABET A TO Z
Color the drawing and trace the letter

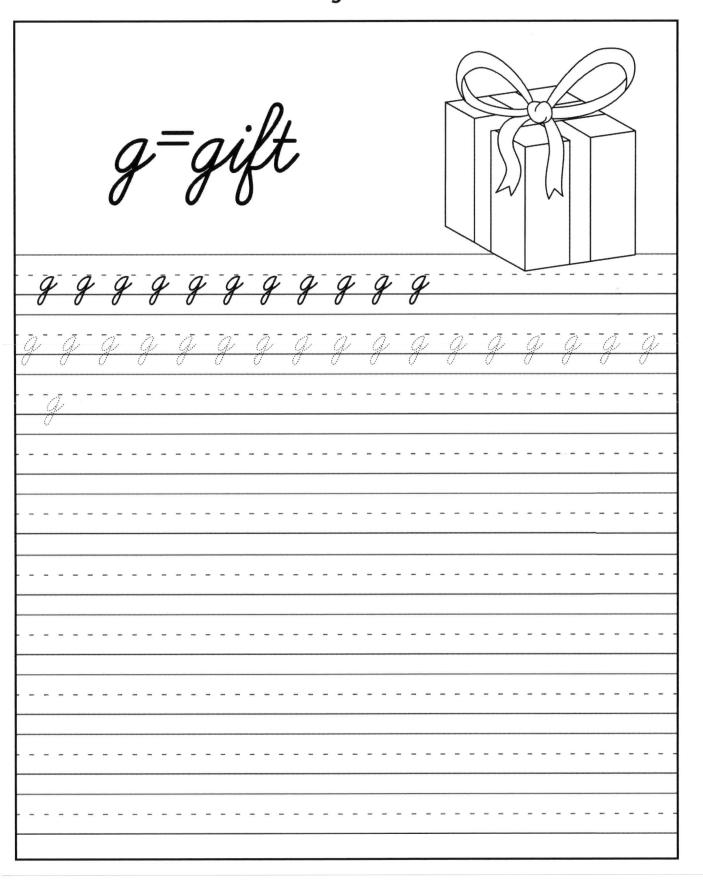

g=gift

ALPHABET A TO Z
Color the drawing and trace the letter

H=House

H H H H H H H H

H H H H H H H H H H H H H

H

ALPHABET A TO Z
Color the drawing and trace the letter

h=house

h h h h h h h h h

h h h h h h h h h h h h h h h h h h

h

ALPHABET A TO Z
Color the drawing and trace the letter

I=Ice cream

I I I I I I I I I I

I I I I I I I I I I I I I I I

I

ALPHABET A TO Z
Color the drawing and trace the letter

i=ice cream

i i i i i i i i i i i i i

i i i i i i i i i i i i i i i i i i i i

i

ALPHABET A TO Z
Color the drawing and trace the letter

J = Jar

ALPHABET A TO Z
Color the drawing and trace the letter

j = jar

j j j j j j j j j j j j

j j j j j j j j j j j j j j j j j j

j

ALPHABET A TO Z
Color the drawing and trace the letter

K=Key

K K K K K K K K K K

K K K K K K K K K K K K K

K

ALPHABET A TO Z

Color the drawing and trace the letter

k=key

k k k k k k k k k k k

k k k k k k k k k k k k k k k k k k k

k

Color the drawing and trace the letter

$L = Light$

L L L L L L L L L L L L

L L L L L L L L L L L L L L

L

ALPHABET A TO Z
Color the drawing and trace the letter

l = light

l l l l l l l l l l l l l l l

l l l l l l l l l l l l l l l l l l l l l l l l

l

ALPHABET A TO Z
Color the drawing and trace the letter

M=Mango

m m m m m m m

m m m m m m m m m m

m

ALPHABET A TO Z
Color the drawing and trace the letter

m = mango

m m m m m m m m

m m m m m m m m m m m m m

m

Color the drawing and trace the letter

n=Notepad

n n n n n n n n n

n n n n n n n n n n n n n n

n

ALPHABET A TO Z
Color the drawing and trace the letter

n = notepad

n n n n n n n n n n

m m m m m m m m m m m m m m m m m m

m

ALPHABET A TO Z

Color the drawing and trace the letter

𝒪=Orange

𝒪 𝒪 𝒪 𝒪 𝒪 𝒪 𝒪 𝒪 𝒪

ALPHABET A TO Z
Color the drawing and trace the letter

o=orange

o o o o o o o o o o o

o o o o o o o o o o o o o o o o o o o o o

o

Color the drawing and trace the letter

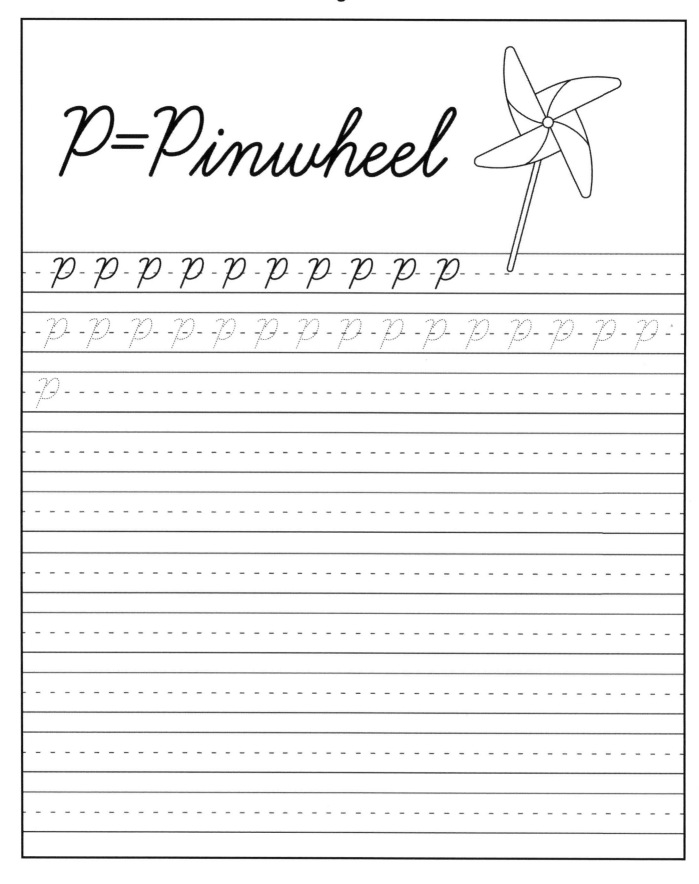

P=Pinwheel

p p p p p p p p p p

p p p p p p p p p p p p p p p p p

p

ALPHABET A TO Z
Color the drawing and trace the letter

p=pinwheel

p p p p p p p p p p

p p p p p p p p p p p p p p

p

ALPHABET A TO Z

Color the drawing and trace the letter

2=Question

?

2 2 2 2 2 2 2 2 2 2

2 2 2 2 2 2 2 2 2 2 2 2 2 2 2 2

2

ALPHABET A TO Z
Color the drawing and trace the letter

q=question

?

g g g g g g g g g g g g g

g g g g g g g g g g g g g g g g g g g

g

R=Rose

RRRRRRRRRRR

RRRRRRRRRRRRR

R

ALPHABET A TO Z
Color the drawing and trace the letter

r = rose

n n n n n n n n n n n n

n n n n n n n n n n n n n n n n

n

ALPHABET A TO Z
Color the drawing and trace the letter

S = Strawberry

S S S S S S S S S S S

S S S S S S S S S S S S S S

S

ALPHABET A TO Z
Color the drawing and trace the letter

s=strawberry

ALPHABET A TO Z
Color the drawing and trace the letter

$T = Tree$

T T T T T T T T T T T T

T T T T T T T T T T T T T T T T T T T T

T

ALPHABET A TO Z
Color the drawing and trace the letter

t=tree

t t t t t t t t t t t t t

t t t t t t t t t t t t t t t t t t t t t

t

Color the drawing and trace the letter

U=Umbrella

U U U U U U U U U U

U U U U U U U U U U U U U U U U

U

ALPHABET A TO Z
Color the drawing and trace the letter

u = umbrella

Color the drawing and trace the letter

$V=Vase$

$V\ V\ V\ V\ V\ V\ V\ V\ V\ V$

$V\ V\ V\ V\ V\ V\ V\ V\ V\ V\ V\ V\ V\ V\ V\ V$

V

ALPHABET A TO Z
Color the drawing and trace the letter

v = vase

Color the drawing and trace the letter

$W=$

Watermelon

W W W W W W W

W W W W W W W W W W W

W

ALPHABET A TO Z
Color the drawing and trace the letter

$w=$

watermelon

w w w w w w w w w

w w w w w w w w w w w w w w

w

ALPHABET A TO Z
Color the drawing and trace the letter

X = Xylophone

X X X X X X X X X X X

X X X X X X X X X X X X X X X

X

ALPHABET A TO Z
Color the drawing and trace the letter

x = xylophone

x x x x x x x x x x x x

x x x x x x x x x x x x x x x x

x

Color the drawing and trace the letter

ALPHABET A TO Z
Color the drawing and trace the letter

y = yoyo

y y y y y y y y y y

y y y y y y y y y y y y y y y

y

ALPHABET A TO Z
Color the drawing and trace the letter

Z = Zipper

Z Z Z Z Z Z Z Z Z

Z Z Z Z Z Z Z Z Z Z Z Z

Z

ALPHABET A TO Z
Color the drawing and trace the letter

z = zipper

Uppercase Cursive Letters

$\mathcal{A}$ a $\mathcal{B}$ $\mathcal{B}$ $\mathcal{C}$ $\mathcal{C}$ $\mathcal{D}$ $\mathcal{D}$

$\mathcal{E}$ $\mathcal{E}$ $\mathcal{F}$ $\mathcal{F}$ $\mathcal{G}$ $\mathcal{G}$ $\mathcal{H}$ $\mathcal{H}$

$\mathcal{I}$ $\mathcal{I}$ $\mathcal{J}$ $\mathcal{J}$ $\mathcal{K}$ $\mathcal{K}$ $\mathcal{L}$ $\mathcal{L}$

$\mathcal{M}$ $\mathcal{M}$ $\mathcal{N}$ $\mathcal{N}$ $\mathcal{O}$ $\mathcal{O}$ $\mathcal{P}$ $\mathcal{P}$

$\mathcal{Q}$ $\mathcal{Q}$ $\mathcal{R}$ $\mathcal{R}$ $\mathcal{S}$ $\mathcal{S}$ $\mathcal{T}$ $\mathcal{T}$

$\mathcal{U}$ $\mathcal{U}$ $\mathcal{V}$ $\mathcal{V}$ $\mathcal{W}$ $\mathcal{W}$ $\mathcal{X}$ $\mathcal{X}$

$\mathcal{Y}$ $\mathcal{Y}$ $\mathcal{Z}$ $\mathcal{Z}$

Lowercase Cursive Letters

a a b b c c d d

e e f f g g h h

i i j j k k l l

m m n n o o p p

q q r r s s t t

u u v v w w x x

y y z z

DAYS OF THE WEEK

Sunday *Sunday*

Monday *Monday*

Tuesday *Tuesday*

Wednesday *Wednesday*

Thursday *Thursday*

Friday *Friday*

Saturday *Saturday*

PRACTICE PAGE
Trace the word

NUMBERS

One One

Two Two

Three Three

Four Four

Five Five

Six Six

Seven Seven

Eight Eight

Nine Nine

Ten Ten

PRACTICE PAGE
Trace the word

ANIMALS

Cat *Cat*

Dog *Dog*

Bird *Bird*

Lizard *Lizard*

Horse *Horse*

Zebra *Zebra*

Fish *Fish*

Snake *Snake*

Rabbit *Rabbit*

Cow *Cow*

PRACTICE PAGE
Trace the word

FRUITS

apple *apple*

pineapple *pineapple*

fig *fig*

peach *peach*

orange *orange*

mango *mango*

banana *banana*

grape *grape*

cherry *cherry*

strawberry *strawberry*

PRACTICE PAGE
Trace the word

SIZE

small small

medium medium

large large

grand grand

tiny tiny

massive massive

average average

big big

little little

petite petite

SPEED

Quick Quick

quick quick

Slow Slow

slow slow

Fast Fast

fast fast

SENTENCE PRACTICE

The five boxing wizards jumped quickly.

The five boxing wizards jumped quickly.

The five boxing wizards jumped quickly.

PRACTICE PAGE
Trace the sentence

SENTENCE PRACTICE

School is closed for the holiday.

School is closed for the holiday.

School is closed for the holiday.

SENTENCE PRACTICE

Please wait until the end to ask questions

Please wait until the end to ask questions.

Please wait until the end to ask questions.

PRACTICE PAGE

PRACTICE PAGE

PRACTICE PAGE

PRACTICE PAGE

PRACTICE PAGE

PRACTICE PAGE

PRACTICE PAGE

PRACTICE PAGE

PRACTICE PAGE

PRACTICE PAGE

PRACTICE PAGE

PRACTICE PAGE

PRACTICE PAGE

PRACTICE PAGE

PRACTICE PAGE

PRACTICE PAGE

PRACTICE PAGE

PRACTICE PAGE

PRACTICE PAGE

PRACTICE PAGE

PRACTICE PAGE

PRACTICE PAGE

PRACTICE PAGE

PRACTICE PAGE

PRACTICE PAGE

PRACTICE PAGE

PRACTICE PAGE

PRACTICE PAGE

PRACTICE PAGE

PRACTICE PAGE

PRACTICE PAGE

PRACTICE PAGE

PRACTICE PAGE

PRACTICE PAGE

PRACTICE PAGE

PRACTICE PAGE

PRACTICE PAGE

PRACTICE PAGE

PRACTICE PAGE

PRACTICE PAGE

PRACTICE PAGE

PRACTICE PAGE

PRACTICE PAGE

PRACTICE PAGE

PRACTICE PAGE

PRACTICE PAGE

Made in the USA
Coppell, TX
13 December 2022

89207620R00061